On Becoming
a Fish

For my mother,
also a walker at the shore.

Emily Hinshelwood
On Becoming a Fish

SEREN

Seren is the book imprint of
Poetry Wales Press Ltd.
57 Nolton Street, Bridgend, Wales, CF31 3AE
www.serenbooks.com
Facebook: facebook.com/SerenBooks
Twitter: @SerenBooks

ISBN: 978-1-85411-577-5

A CIP record for this title is available from the British Library.

The publisher acknowledges the financial assistance of the Welsh Books Council.

Cover art: Angela Lutz c/o www.wizeyez

Printed in Bembo by the Berforts Group Ltd, Stevenage.

Contents

Sandscape After Hours

Amroth

Each footprint a journey
turns the beach into dreamtime.

They collide, converge
in silent riot of unmet strangers:

perhaps a supple body twisting,
flicking sand wishes to the wind

or two minds in opposition
slinging firm prints in terse lines

and there, a loner shuffles
an exotic weft into the mesh
then falters.

The sun's glance burns
into the depth of every step

every pattern of feet on sand,
each strand weaving dreamfibres

without start or end
just journeys

and
sweet sea havoc on the turn.

Westphalian

Wiseman's Bridge

The rocks have worn to a sauna of bodies
draped irreverently across the shore.

There is no thought, amongst these grey masses,
for sleekness. The beauty is in bulges and creases.

Sun drags over bellies, hot breasts
tummyholes crammed with small stones

and bits of crab. They are idle. Exude heat.
Oblivious to the chopper grinding overhead.

They glow. In the grand scheme of things
they have seen mountains swell, crack, twist

erode. They know the wind will change.
They know they will clasp rigid, naked,

cold, as the sea rolls over their heads.

Lady Cave Anticline

Saundersfoot

*Anticline − an arch or upfold in rocks, generally produced by the
bending upwards of rock beds under pressure from the sides.*

He's bowing to her all the way from the harbour
head down, eyes lowered, every pace along the beach
bending to a shell to smell its scent, then casting it off
if it's not divine enough.

She is still relatively young,
though pressured on all sides
forced to bend and arch.
Those that lay on her have gone,
and she is stiff as whalebone.

He moves in slow silence until he picks a yellow cone shell,
still glistening. He sniffs it, flicks his tongue to taste its ridges,
feels with large fingers the tiny aperture, the shiny liplike columella,
then he strides to Lady Cave Anticline.

She has never had such a visitor.
All others have gawped at her broken spine,
tossed theories like a ball
measured, scraped,
talked about her.

He gently rubs a small hole into her tight, stressed folds,
makes such exquisite strokes the weight of millennia eases.
He pushes in the yellow shell, slightly hidden. Whispers.
Then walks towards the headland and disappears.

Mrs Cheveley in the Conservatory at Tenby

Tenby

*as suggested by Oscar Wilde in 'An Ideal Husband' in which
Mrs Cheveley says "and you threw me over because you saw,
or said you saw, poor old Lord Mortlake trying to have a violent
flirtation with me in the conservatory at Tenby".*

Whether it was true or not about the violent flirtations,
Mrs C. was sticking to her story. And that's that.

She had a sweet sleightful smile
like the sugar-glazed pastel shades of this town –
we all adore it, even though we know
that pirates have infested its undergarments.

The rain that day would have whipped Wesley
from his box, she said. It slapped against the glass in sheets.

And from behind she felt his breath upon her neck
like the wind on the Dead House Steps.
No, it was worse, she said, it was like the acid
that strips ulcerous sores.

She might have cowered like boats in the harbour,
knocking with fright.

But Mrs. C was not to be violated.
She simply turned, pecked him on the cheek,
then made her way to the Castle Keep
where she fiddled with the sunshine meter.

When the rays were full, glowing and blazing with heat,
she rolled out her bathing machine and ran long-knickered
into the sea.

The Goldfish

Caldey Island

We came by boat to this holy rock.
We're permitted a stroll: the chocolatery,
the perfumery, the old priory
where a girl is writing *Lord, help my Goldfish.*

She smoothes her prayer with reverence,
then her parents lead her away.

A woman has fallen to her knees.
She is wailing "Jesus Jesus".
The girl's prayer is filed in a stack
for delivery. We watch Mass

from the gallery.
The brothers file in, in simple cloth.

The video says
Brother X left the army,
Brother Y left his stress,
and all our donations help
in this crossing of the sea,

this theatre of habits,
these meals in silence.

Seduction

Skrinkle Haven

You came across it lying on the track
slightly kinked on a chink of sun
diamonds lined all down its back.

Your first snake.

You crouched at the verge,
reached your finger, felt it stir
watched it lift its head,
picked it whole upon your hand –

the untouchable touched.
How were you to know it was an adder?
And would knowing have stopped you?

Lady in White

Manorbier

(for Rachael)

Lady in White is a young woman ghost who can sometimes
be seen drifting along the coast of Pembrokeshire.

I think of her as music played by two flutes
in some cluttered pocket of our school,
the pencilled marks of key changes, sharps and notes
to start, stop. And at night (the polished silver packed up)
us giggling over a missed breath: a duet that stretches
in echoes to us here on this slab of rock.

She appears now amongst these teens
clustered round fires in the bay. Their flames
suck the entire heat from the sky. We swig
from a hipflask, flex our fingers in quick arpeggios.
Words crack out in staccato: the cold, the headland,
the tide on the turn and with it, stretched across the horizon

the tune from that duet we always used to play.

Skinny Dipping

Swanlake Bay

I've not seen a soul all day,
so, pinky-naked,
I clamber over slabs of swirly sandstone
noting how the tide
has made seats for mermaids.

The water is champagne-cold
and burns all the way up.
With a fizz
all the bitty thoughts of the morning
spill into the sea.

I pull back out
and slip ungainly on the rocks
flinging my arms out star-shaped
blushing *in toto*
checking the bay instinctively...

there, on a rock sits
a man – his head plunged
firmly in a book. He doesn't look
but as I pass, I see
he's also naked, and blushing

his bottle of Fanta strategically placed.

First Flight

Swanlake Bay

(for Kani)

You decided to have a go at flying,
rigged up a rickety kitchen chair
with a kind of parachute tied to its back bars.

In the shallow waves, the wind launched you up
suddenly tilting, tipping the seat back and forth.

We watched from the beach as your wobbling frame
went higher and higher till you were so far off
you could fit like a bug on the tip of my finger.

> *No safety belt*
> > *No harness.*

I kept you there, moving my finger up in the air
as your body grew smaller and smaller.

Beetle – ladybird – sandhopper – flea.

When everyone else went back to cooking sausages
and building sandcastles, I had to stay there, still,
with my finger out like a living statue

in case I was the only thing that kept you
from falling out of the sky and into the sea.

Edge

Trewent

1.
My favourite lecturer used to slide
through the department in his Inuit socks,
at parties wouldn't realise he was theorising
with his wine glass on his head.
"Change," he always said, "happens at the edge,
the frontline, tideline, the thick line
that sparks a fight and then, perhaps,
a kiss. This is where we know who we are"
he said, "by seeing who we are not".

2.
Along the boundary hedge
is a thick border of chatter:
dragonflies skim through symphonies of flowers.
A touching racket of glitz-bugs,
bumbles backing out of foxgloves,
helicoptering away. Canvassing.
Bartering. A market of all-sorts,
poking out sloes, haws, handfuls of
who-will-buy-my-sweet-red-roses?

3.
But here, there's just a twisted wire, spiked,
catching farmers' plastic. A flagging daisy
chokes on bindweed. A sign – *Keep Out* –
is raw and stark. A law in black and white.
Galvanized. And now it's everywhere: razor wire,
electric fences. We make our way around them,
trailing like herds
                    like souls split from our minds,
no longer knowing if we are inside or out.

First Baron Cawdor of Castlemartin

Stackpole

God knows how you bribed your peerage!
Services to Pitt? Or was it chocolate house chat
that got you sat so squat on this bit of cracked ocean?

So, you dug lily ponds, hollowed a quay
juxtaposed genteel lakes with the hammering
sea, gazed on pink petals when all around

the price of barley was just out of reach.
Nothing wears out a fine face like democracy.
Lilies outgrow Lords. They still open flowers

to damselflies as the world shifts in the sky.
A court toppled to stones, a threadbare coat of arms,
crinolined ladies in Barafundle Bay...

And now? They are all just sand on the Warren.

Stack Rock

Elegug Stacks

One step closer to the edge. It is heavy quiet.
Scrub. Horseflies pierce my legs.
Tiny serrated swords. It is hot sticky.
I slap them. Dead. A sign of a man falling
off the cliff. One could trip.

One more step and silence breaks.
Guillemots, auks jostle on a rock stack.
They shuffle, yawk, mew, howl.
They dive hurling their weight.
They scream into crags.

There is hopefulness in this chaos,
packed on this rock island,
this disorderly waiting, this
sitting it out, this shrieking protest
on a stack at the edge of the coast.

Looking for Glow-worms

Freshwater West

After three years of developing as larvae, adult glow-worms
live for only 8 or 9 days. Females attract a mate by emitting a light
from luminous organs on the underside of their tail segments.

In the burrows the sea is hushed
under a tinnitus of crickets
the occasional snap-thump, grey-black.
In the dense willow thicket
a crunch of snails, sea-spurge.
The thin moon is a hairline crack.

Paths in the marram grass
are the manic criss-crosses
of lost souls. There are holes
large enough for small corpses.
Four names are marked in the sand.
The rib-cage of a bird.

Looking till half-blind –
but not a segment
not a spark, not a pinprick
of light in the shadows
where the sea meets the dark.

Then, driving home on midnight roads
everything glows: white crates, lamp-posts,
vans in driveways… and beyond the ridge
white floodlights on the oil refinery.

A Las Vegas of glow-worms!

Bubblepop and the Devil's Balls

Gravel Bay

They're firing today
flying the red flags
provoking my bullish streak:
Do not touch any military debris –
it may explode and kill you.

But their bubblepop has no grit
they're spitting peas
when they could be hurling
the devil's balls into the sea
I'd like that... today.

Today, everything is too calm,
the sea too blue,
the heather pert and pink
the clouds are wispy.
Wispy!

Old foxgloves are nodding like neighbours
chin-wagging over the hedge.
The path sundays along the beach
the waves check in orderly,
one by one.

Then, I discover Gravel Bay,
I tuck in among black grumpy rocks
sulking in the shallows
I unwrap my lunch.
Fucking lovely.

Handover

Rat Island

There is a profound change taking place.
The sun, pink from the exercise of the day
is exhausted, ready to dip into the horizon.
Just me and thirty-odd sea birds perched
on matchlegs stare out at the bleeding sky.
Behind us the moon, a perfect tissue circle
is beginning to rise. It is the handover
between separated parents. The child –
hula-hooping – doesn't notice her pink suitcase
moved between cars, or the quiet words
as they watch her hips rhythmically beating,
keeping the spin in balance.
They exchange practicalities, simple messages.
The base of the sun fizzes orange into the sea.
Birds stand till the final moment
in this tiniest of ceremonies.

And the handover is complete, the grass
will loose its redness, the sea will start to shuffle
as the moon, whitening in the purple sky
climbs up through the gears.

Raspberry Ripple

West Angle Bay

In the café a small boy
who's sliced his hand on a washed up razor
is fretting – in floods.

His ice-cream and blood
river down his arm which he licks
between gasps.

His mother on the floor
with napkins, sops the gash
and the café lady calls an ambulance.

An old man props his stick,
tells how he once snapped his leg,
tied it with a washed up scrap of rope
and walked home.

Daughter

Old Point House, Angle
(For Eira)

Until now, I didn't know how dark it was inside.
It seemed a cosy place to have a pint.
The seats are worn and wonky. Torn-up
beer mats wedged under table legs.
On the walls are curiosities: nets, an old clock
whose hands are slow. All the regulars
are talking shop.

You peer in now, nose to the glass,
your hands shield the sun's glare,
your smile as wide as the bay behind,
your eyes are a lighthouse beam
scanning the shadows for me,
rummaging amongst memorabilia
for my shape.

And though I smile and wave
I've ghosted into dust.
You turn from the window,
out of the frame
leaving me low-ceilinged
and cluttered, staring
at the square of light where you had been.

Jetties

Pwllcrochan

Jetties are matchsticks, balanced into piers.
Like card houses, eventually you stack one too many.

A tanker is docking three hundred thousand tons of oil,
ribbed waves rock to shore. Chimneys are belching,
a low hum under the pylon. The air smells of engine.

Everything crackles. Even the trees.
Out of a sycamore, a squirrel plummets
with a loud crack on the tarmac.

In the bay, a single turbine
spins, dizzy with the wind.

Bazaar

Pembroke

Ghosting through the bazaar
to escape the heat, reaching
into bowls of old bullets, eye glasses
that still unfold, wood print blocks,
tins for Oxo, a telescope
that concertinas out to space
and back to a small weight
in your pocket,
there is another woman.

She's wearing my baseball cap
my tie-dye vest,
the same detached expression
on her face. She reaches slowly
to open a box –
a hall of mirrors.
Our profiles pass at corners
multiplied then distorted,
stretched from each other

till we are so thin
and so far
we form a single unending line.

Beetroot

Under the Cleddau Bridge

The two swans had been floating
like love letters, open only to each other.
When I threw in a lump of my sandwich
I caught one of them on the back of the head.

Beetroot is rich in iron and the bread was dense.
Sandwich? More like being hit by a rock.
Its mate turned, dragged itself from the water
with an air of urban wisdom

one large webbed foot at a time
into knee-high sludge
the swamp sucking back
sharp intakes of breath

slap left
slap right.

It stepped measuredly
over a taut chain.
Its feathers were not white.
They were rust-stained.

It loomed at me
I yielded my last piece
I splayed my hands
to make it understand

It knelt back into the water.
It lifted its beak.
It offered the beetroot to its mate
and they glided on upriver.

I.K. Brunel

Neyland

As a boy, he tried to look big
on his little pony. Sitting tall,
ballooning his lungs.
Kingdom.

He was the tiny cog
that set their whole thing
in motion.
Steam Child.

He rattled
at twenty times the speed,
he defied the night
in his 'flying hearse',
swung in a basket
high above the Avon
to fix a kink in the cable.

Life was mechanical then
puff and pistons
cranks and winches
winding, grinding, spinning smaller
smaller, twist
slot, shunt, kick
hisssss
    till the whole world
    was so tiny
    it slipped into their pockets
    like a marble.

They buried him.
A poor man
in a small grave.

Maritime Museum

Milford Haven

He used to be a fisherman: dragged nets
as the moon drags water, hauling all manner of life
from the sea, knew the sweep of the ocean,
still bobs with it now, as he steers through caverns
thick with history. You could get lodged in here and grow.

He's worried about the lights, wants it bright
to see the ice factory, silver floods of hake,
herrings packed in baskets.
The sperm whale is so large it could sink a fleet
but is alarmed by a bird landing on its back.

Upstairs, I'm plunged into blackness.
Nelson vanishes along with war maps of the Haven,
the Quakers, the sunk *Lusitania*.
Every crude oil refinery is put out instantly.
I collide with cabinets, batting for a light switch.

When they flicker back on there are whalers
stabbing at a calf. A ship full of blubber and blood.
They're wading in vats of whale oil for the lights of London.
The great mother hangs at a distance calling
until they take her too in the thick of her loss.

On Becoming a Fish

Milford Haven

Tales of the sea didn't prepare me for this.
It all seemed so Jack Sparrow, so Barti Du,
perhaps a mermaid flung on a rock,
whales. Jonah.
You know what I mean.
Even the fish stall with its ice trays
and neat lines of flat eyes, even he spins yarns
as he slices heads into a bucket.

When you stop coming up for air,
when your lungs implode to a stillness
all that talking ceases.
All that *endless* talking.
And you half-remember poking
at a lobster with rubberbanded claws
noting how prehistoric it was
and someone said something about the future.

Sounds now are just noise
against my body.
This is my story.
I keep telling it over and over.
For it's just me
defying gravity.
The swish of my tail
darting.

It's starting to feel like I'm dancing.

Dale Field Studies

Dale

They're out early at the shore
in yellow macs, fleece hats,
peering close at razorshells,
tight-knitted mussels
on a washed up buoy, crabs,
they poke at piles of kelp, flip
a dead dogfish and other sea-kill
from the choppy night before.

They work alone, move
low to the ground, observe
calcium patterns, barnacle plates,
mouths of brittle stars, make notes.
Every now and then, one calls out.
A cluster forms like a bracelet
of bright beads. Then it spills apart
as though the twine is cut.

At the far end, two girls crouch
making small offerings of shells
to each other. Heads now touch,
now part. They inch forward,
exchange words. At a rock pool
they remove gloves, dip their hands.
Then stand and look out at the horizon
one hugging the other from behind.

Wreck

Mill Bay

HMS Barking *sank in Mill Bay on*
March 14th 1964 during a force 6 gale.

After its collapse, the body
was left exposed, rusting
in the bay, photographed
and inspected by people
who pass. The occasional
moan as water gushed in
and out.

Twice daily it is bathed
by the sea. Sand settles
like blankets. Sequins
of limpets, barnacles.
Salt cuts lacework as
the stiff body is eroded rib
by rib.

It is sewn into the rocks.
Embroidered.
Decorated.

Buried.
Until the bay
just breathes
ship.

And,
without knowing why,
a woman picnicking here
dreams
of sailing away.

Intent

Westdale Bay

In this puddle, stretched right to left
across the sand, blue sky is reflected.
White clouds hare over the ground.
A girl splashes through air
her plaits swinging.
She picks her feet up high
as though the clouds
are catching in her toes.

She trails thongweed,
writes her name
like a statement of intent.
Each letter is absorbed
into the sky. And, as though
in reply, hundreds of jellyfish
glisten in the ridges

like stars dropped down to earth.

Driftwood

Marloes

A huge plank has washed up,
wedged flat onto boulders
on the beach.

It is a giant spirit level
from God's toolbox
put here to gauge a dying faith
against His targets for the week.

Some say He's discarded it in disgust
at being forced to apply for his own job
to prove himself by taking NVQs
in Peace, Planning and Publicity.

The job always gave him such pleasure
a sense of worth. It was his lifeline.

He may take to drink
lose parts of his mind
talk all the time about
"those seven great days".

But you'd stop to listen,
wouldn't you
if you saw Him in a doorway
with a few grubby blankets?

Bird Watching

Skomer Island

My daughter is fascinated by the dead ones:
127 Manx Shearwaters.
But did we need to fork out extra cash for the binoculars?

She tells everyone about our dead bird watching,
points to the scrub and does, in fact, use the binoculars
to see their twisted spinal columns in grotesque detail.

Other visitors think the seals are more rewarding.
They urge us, hand us their very own binoculars
to watch them lounging on rocks – pregnant.

We oblige,
we make the right oohs and ahhs,
then return to our counting.

The Woman at The Lobster Pot

East Hook Farm

grew up in lighthouses and tells us stories
of midnights when ships crashed the rocks
and earthquaked her teddies out of bed,
all the lighthouse families snaking
down to the bay with soup and blankets.

Her father knew the rocks
like his own knuckles,
all his life he watched the beam
for boats, radioed for help.

The Sea Empress *couldn't have happened.*
It strayed and should have been warned.
But they're all automated now. No eyes on the sea.
Just a light on a timer. Broke my father's heart.

Walking back on a moonless night
between dark hedgerows
we are followed by that empty sweeping beam
glancing across us all the way home.

Francess Bevans

St Bride's Haven

Francess Bevans was buried in St Bride's Haven
in 1837, aged 16.

Some say you were threading a daisy chain
when the edge toppled under you.
At its wildest streak it can do that.

Now your stone grave is uplifted by the tide
and who knows, you are dancing the bay,
on the brink of adulthood – forever becoming.

The old fisherman has you in mind
as he picks his way into the chopsing waves.
He's always at the clash of edges, the fringes,

the moment when the mind unhinges.
There he catches pearls, looks to you in heaven
and threads them on a chain – like your daisies.

Mayflowers

Foxes' Holes

The face of Saddam Hussein flaps in a hedge.
He was front page news a few days back and triggers
a memory of the edge of Iraq lined with mines
and horizons of Kurds clamouring to leave.

Now, his head is pinned by hawthorn.
He half-breathes through gulps of wind.
He will loosen eventually and sog
alongside fag packets and Tesco bags.

Mayflowers will blossom.
Daisies will spring up like freckles.
and close-up in the rocks
you will see glints of quartz and spots of garnet.

Unexpectedly

Newgale

(for Phillip Cockwell)

My friend will die today. Unexpectedly.
But for now, there is still a breeze.

Across the beach, people stretch out on towels.
Roasting. A lizard vanishes across the track.

The ground is hard-trodden, cracked,
speckled with sun-hats and walking poles.

Somewhere further up there is a hole.
        A wall of flowers nodding.

I cut from the path, scratch through brambles,
clamber over boulders. Ease into the sea.

Ferns uncurl. No faster, no slower.
Just as they always have done.

I am caught by a column of flat stones
balanced precariously.

The breeze has stopped.
I place a single white rock on the top.

Porpoise Washed Up

Broad Haven

I could be writing of its boldness
its exhilarating freedom.
The use of rubber flesh, unzipped,
is so intense the eye flinches from it.

The thick buzzing of bluebottles
lends a further twist.
The energy is hectic.
We are delightfully unsettled.

We have to imagine the hook –
and all the other creatures
who have been cut up with equal flair
with equal ingenuity.

Did Cavemen Build Sandcastles?

Druidston

Did cavemen build sandcastles,
carve buckets from fresh oak, spades
from great grandma's pelvic bone?

Did they dig sandcaves? Wedge bits
of washed-up wood as pit props,
with their blood imprint wild stallions,
rummage through flotsam,
pick out old teeth and broken antlers?

Did they stay up all night, all week? Roast a boar
propped between rocks over one helluva fire
and tear into fat-spitting hunks of pork?
Dance under *our* crescent moon
with nothing on? *Nothing.* Then shriek
into waves and surf on their bellies?

Did they dream up sand-cities
people hopping like sandflies
scurrying between floors of vast sand towers
and juggernauts that bark along motorways

then let the tide wash them away?

Pen Dinas

Pen Dinas

From the south it has the girth
of a slumped horse – dead in childbirth.
Jaw pressed to water. Chilled. Stiff.

Splashes of foam float at the head.
There is a hiss, a breathy heat.
A deep inhalation, then, release.

The horse-rock starts to crack,
lurch forward, stagger to its feet
to pull from the sea its dripping hide,

to lift the coast onto its back,
to bellow a full mania, and charge,
dragging the world's carpet out of the bay.

On the Gribbin

Solva

She's talking to herself again
up on the headland, mouthing off
amongst the cows on the Gribbin.

Even the crows bark and lift
as every exclamation mark
hammers at the cliff.

Below, a boat zigzags in the water,
with sails up like a butterfly
it heads for The Smalls,

where a lighthouse is pinned
to a rock, far off from day trippers,
alone and blinking.

She's spotted a Cabbage White.
She capers across the grass
arms reaching out,

her hands scrubbed raw,
trying to collect back her words,
trying to catch the butterfly.

Searching for a map of Pembrokeshire in Pembrokeshire

Haverfordwest

"I got maps
all sorts of maps
over here
Saxmundham, Wigan Pier...
What d'you say? ... map of Pembrokeshire?
not a lot of call for that round here
not *in* Pembrokeshire
most people know where to go....
No, can't help you there
I got Ipswich if you want,
bit dear – Blackpool, Liverpool, Pontypool
you'll like it there –
got maps coming out of my ears
still fixed on Pembrokeshire?
Oh well, suit yourself
I like the one of Wigan pier myself."

Wishing Well

St Non's Bay

This poem was written during an adjournment
of a public inquiry about a community-wind farm,
Awel Aman Tawe, near Swansea.

The chamber is stale with dead breath
arguing "yes wind farm", "no wind farm"
stale with "climate change poo poo"
with "nobody has a right to mess with *my* view"
with "what about the dead poet who
loved this spot?"

The chamber is stale with mud-stuck plod –
with "windfarms look like bog brushes –
kill our birds, sheep, horses, fish and children"
with "windfarms bring the psychos out"
with "windfarms look like manic crucifixions
and don't forget what happened to Jesus".

So, let's throw a penny into Non's Well –
after all, she gave us David
perhaps she'll sort out climate change as well.

Great Bitch of Ramsey Sound

Pen Dal Aderyn

It was years ago he hit her
smack in the face
she happened to be in the wrong place
at the wrong time
still coping
phantom nursing
minding her own
when he lurched stern first
cracked his hull against her girth
tossed at the tide
wits wild and undone
till he washed up at the pub
downed a round of jibe-talking
jeering *where's your balls boy?*
and he called her *Great Bitch.*

I didn't stop him
thought it would blow over
gulped beer
one ear to the crowd
that was puffed and roused
I shrank into the smoke
didn't know the name would stick
didn't know the shame
would keep me quiet
didn't know the years they would goad
and hound her.

Sometimes I hear her howl
now split in two
and I whisper into the Sound
Myfanwy
I still remember your name.

Kyrie Eleison

St David's Cathedral

"Lord, have mercy"

Once the angelic mass had softened us
we were invited into strangers' conversations,
forgave the priest his quick fag in the cloisters,
his wonky dog collar, him swaying back to his seat.
After the crescendos had opened us like buds
unfolding throughout the cathedral
and we cried out when the bass fell from the choir
and the paramedics wheeled in the chair.

Afterwards, softened, opened, we bowed out
into the bucketing rain, cranked up our hoods,
unleashed umbrellas… The lead violinist ducked
out the back, scurried up the steps, his tails flapping.
With a curt nod, he pipped his car alarm and sped
up the drive drenching everyone at the side of the road.

Coetan Arthur Burial Chamber

St David's Head

Bulges of gabbro elbow out of the ground,
coarse-grained lumps of limbs shoved out
blown off, slowly erode into mud–flesh,

the world slices you to your knees
till you crawl, half human,
creak like cracked ice,

a line of ribs is exposed
and this giant capstone cranked up
wedged on an upright leads straight to the dead.

You are given sea-spurrey, thrift, stonecrop —
flowers that will open when you next decide to speak.

The Purple Sandpipers

Ramsey Island

Out there, tucked on volcanic ledges
like arctic pottery in an earthy shop,
one per shelf, minimalist and raw.
They lay their eggs on high rocks,
in damp basements. Migrants
in danger of oil spills, freak waves.

And the young have to feed themselves.

Jetsam

Whitesands Bay

Far-flung exotica
have washed up on the beach.
And so have I
with my courgette pie
and pomegranate juice.
All strange together, we sit.

An orange plastic glove,
half sunk in seaweed tagliatelle
is tangled with fishing line
into a *thumbs up* sign.
I return the gesture,
then check the bay
in case I've been spotted
communing with jetsam.

All over the beach
small shells tug themselves
from wet sand,
drag smartly in silken lines
no roots, no baggage,
just living...
                    till the next tide.

Like those people
picked up by the moon.
They leave their keys,
their kids, no note, no trace,
begin all fresh again
with a new name.

Blue Lagoon

Abereiddy

A duck flaps in and lands ungainly,
legs spreadeagled. It bobs
then, head first, goes under

for whole decades.

It dives down past walls of limpets
'dead man's fingers', spider crabs
anemones,

past galleries of men who blast the rock,
who still crank out blocks of slate,
and bring graptolites to surface again

past quarryboys, slaters
tippers, cutters
past Thomas Thomas
who lodged in The Street
and worked the winding gear,

past the dust,
the grind,
the slate splinters.

But has it gone past the giant Conger Eels
who wheel around and sift history?
Below that, they say, there is no bottom.

Quarry

Porthgain

At times words need helping out,
not savagely, with forceps,
but cut carefully, for they are primeval,
a cluster of feelings, still at risk.
Some don't make it. They haunt you.

Here, simple words in giant letters are laid to rest.
I LOVE YOU cracked from granite
the size of an adult across the quarry floor.
From above, they can be seen growing back
into the hot earth from where words are born.

Halloween in Trefin

Trefin

After a hike, in the Ship Inn,
my body is like the skeleton
in my mother's closet,
strung together with picture wire.

I rub tomato ketchup on my lips,
eyeball a young Dracula,
who runs out crying for mam,
dropping his fangs. I lick my lips.

Three feisty ghouls clatter in
with shredded coats
and pitchforks, giggling
over a packet of lovehearts.

A man with four sparkly tridents
and a horned baby asleep on his arm
shouts "cokes for all the devils",
and aims his credit card at the bar.

Outside, a breeze, stiff from the sea,
whistles through the pallets
of a towering woodstack
in a circle of standing stones.

Bladderwrack

Abercastell

In the bubbles of bladderwrack,
keeping seaweed afloat,
are bygone memories.
They don't pop easily,

but, as the sun slips
down the back of the sea,
try making fire with a bunch
of salt-cracked woodsticks.

Chuck on dried bladderwrack.
When it's popping bullets
out of the fire breathe in
a potpourri of the ocean:

the smell of wrecks, traders,
the stink of whalers, oil spills,
starfish, dogfish, jellyfish,
the breath of saints,

scents dragged
from the ocean floor
and kept
in these pockets of air

intense
sealed inside seaweed,
and now released hot
into this new century.

At the Memorial Stone to Dewi Emrys

Pwll Deri

'a thina'r meddilie sy'n dwad ichi
Pan fo'ch chi'n ishte uwchben Pwllderi'
...and these are the thoughts that will come to you
as you sit above Pwll Deri

Two strangers on a promontory –
bobble-hats, anoraks, wind-filled cheeks
and winter birds low to the ground.
He pulls the entire poem from his bag,
they hold it together to translate
the thoughts above Pwll Deri.

Like skeletal hedges, they rough out
impressions – the sheer bay, steps
hacked through rock. Each offers words – ·
lonely cottage, mother sheep,
poet overrun with memory,
picture on picture till the final page

when they part in opposite ways,
without asking each other's names.

Honeymoon

Strumble Head

We pegged our tent to the scrub
at Strumble Head, a mussel on a rock,
watched the November sun plop into black
and the start of the free star-show.

We wedged the stove out of the wind,
broke veg, threw lentils in, knocked back
red wine from tin mugs, feasted
clad in bobblehats, breathing out fog.

We slid into sleeping bags,
zipped out the world, stuck the bottle
in the tent pocket. In nature's silence
and the blackness of seven o'clock

we braced the first shiver of undressing
and the exquisite search for warmth.

The Last Invasion of Britain, 1797

Carreg Wastad

So,
it was here
at these basalt cliffs
they anchored their ships,
clambered, in balloon trousers,
with grenades and the Tricolores,
planned to strike chaos into the nub
of trade, burning, pillaging, preparing
to incite the poor to rise up and fight.

But they hadn't accounted for
Mrs. Williams' excellent eyesight, or
Jemima Fawr, the last great cobbler,
who single-handedly seized a dozen
soldiers and went back for more, or
four hundred Welsh women wearing
stove-pipe hats and scarlet cloaks
marching dragoon-like to the shore.

So it was here that the revolution
didn't happen, that in the end
the Cawdors and cobblers
rallied together, marched
a thousand Frenchmen,
sick on raw chicken,
drunk on wine
all the way
to jail.

Fishguard Lifeboat Crew

Fishguard

The holy sister is pegging out the convent smalls
into a stiff winter breeze. She stops for a call
on her cellphone. Freezes. Looks to the ocean.

The BT man sits on a stool, in blue dungarees,
stares at yarns of coloured wire that spaghetti
in coils onto the pavement.

The barmaid is pulling pints for regulars
at the Royal Oak. Roger is bringing lobsters
onto the harbour in net baskets.

At the lunchtime showing at Theatre Gwaun,
a lad watches Pirates of the Caribbean
his long legs cramped up like a spider.

Steve has piled his frozen meals on the conveyor
at the Co-op, Doc steps out of the shower
reaches for a towel....

At sea, a flare goes up.
The shout goes out. Bleeps
on the wrists of the lifeboat crew.

Dusk Chorus

Cwm yr Eglwys

There will come a moment
when the birds stop singing.

For now, they are loud, shrill,
begging the sun to shine.

While there is light,
they keep catching flies,

but when dusk turns,
something dies.

Their songs are scattered gems,
they've lost the tightness of morning,

excitement dissolves into panic
as blackness haunts.

When light is finally taken,
there is silence from the treetops

all silhouettes are lost
to the night.

Crossing the Estuary

Nevern Estuary

(for Mary Walters)

When the police went in, they found
eggs wedged on rafters in his attic:
rare crows, ospreys, golden eagles
unhatched in cracks and gaps in the ceiling

two thousand eggs stored like a stamp collection

not a twitter, not a hoot, no warbles
no squeals, no skimming on the water
no trills, no clap-chattering on the mudflats
no swooping on the air or gliding or weaving

just silence,
and the occasional gurgle of his central heating.

Boat

Newport

The air is winter thin,
sounds of birds
run like wet paint
across the sky.

A boat emerges
from the bank
as one might
from a dream

or a creature
shrugging off
hibernation

easing its bowlshape
out of the reeds
brushing off mildew.

With no-one in the seat
it pulls out rotting oars
damp, worm eaten

rows
past the Parrog
and creaks out
into the Celtic Sea.

The Golf Course

The Bennet

I still blame the concussion –
the cold crack of the bike rack to my skull.
I'm mixing words, told the girls
I'd buy them skirts in Lebanon,
stole a whole trolley by mistake
and have to keep checking I'm not naked.

Here, there's no-one else walking.
No-one to staple me to reality.
There are cracks, rips, slips,
so the line-ups don't match.
Birds cry out of thin air,
giant mackerel perch on their fins.
There are bones on the path – I'm almost certain
they're not mine.

And now on the brow, in the mist
men dragging bodies from ditches,
shoulders hunched in silent howling
Pushing. Pulling. Bent to task and ghost
choirs breaking our hearts with all those
war songs our parents used to sing.

There'll be blue birds.

A flight of steps is sliced into the hill
I'm counting myself like a register
until I've reassembled sense into me,
look back through the gorse at the golf course
and there's a raven on the fence singing
tomorrow, just you wait and see.

Malleus Maleficarum
(The Hammer of Witches, 1486)

Witches Cauldron

Once the damned handbook had been written
and the god squad snapped into battle
with their finger breakers and the ducking stools
the gendercide began: herbalists, midwives,
wise old women licking and blistering, skin
popping, hair catching like dried bracken....

Those that escaped packed into the moon
like forming a ball of pastry. It is rolled and cut.
Rolled and cut, while on and on the hurley burley:
women rupturing inside out; strong girls
lashed, electric bolts shot through their heads.
A dead badger is slumped like a blooded coat.

A parcel of oystercatchers launches into the sky,
vanishes on a turn. Another appears as if from tomorrow.

The moon keeps pulling the tide.
It is rolled and cut, rolled and cut.

Final walk

St Dogmaels

The Globemaker stands
with rows of still worlds
waiting to roll from the workshop.
She sets one spinning:
porpoises, guillemots,
a clattering of choughs
spilling into the sky
oceans of waves,
a merry hell of rattlesnakes.
Somewhere a god
tempting us to delirium.

And in a box, the stuff of reality —
the patchwork of history
sewn into a picnic
of well-worn stories
all these myths we keep moving
hand to hand,
thought to thought
before the spell breaks,
red, white shells scatter,
and the evolutionary ladder collapses
to way back before we were monkeys

costumes vanish, mammoth tusks
ammonites, all those saints shrunk up
kaleidoscoping inwards
sucked back one inside the other
dissolving into water
till it's nothing but atoms, cells
a molecule of a tear on an eye
that miraculously
for one expanded moment
held the power
to imagine.

Acknowledgements

Acknowledgements are due to the editors of the following journals where some of these poems first appeared:
Acumen, Aesthetica Creative Works Annual, Artemis, Boomslang, Cadenza, Cambria: National Magazine of Wales, The Interpreter's House, The Long Islander, The Moth, The New Welsh Review, Poetry Wales, The Rialto, Roundyhouse, Staple.

And in the following anthologies:
'Sandscape After Hours': *Fragments from the Dark* (Hafan Books).
'Frances Bevans'*: In the Telling* (Cinnamon Press).
'Malleus Maleficarum 1486', 'At the Momorial Stone to Dewi Emrys':
The Voice of Women in Wales (Wales Women's National Coalition).

'Haymaking' and 'Bladderwrack' were exhibited on Arriva buses in commemoration of Darwin bicentenary.

There is a video of 'Lady Cave Anticline' on www.poetryvlog.com.

'Blue Lagoon' and 'Crossing the Estuary' have both won first prize in a Friends of the Earth competition.

I would also like to thank the following friends, family and colleagues: Anna Smith, Sally Spedding, Marion Preece, Hillary Wickers, Beth Morgan, Sandra Mackness for their regular and invaluable critical feedback, Paul Henry for his sensitive and focused criticism, Jeni Williams for her critical support, Literature Wales for their financial help, Mum and Nick, Dad and Gillian, Anna and Paul for all having faith in me, Amy Wack for her invaluable support and enthusiasm, and mostly to Dan, Kani and Eira for their constant love and acceptance.